The White Bridge

♓

Francine Sterle

$5.95
ISBN: 1-886895-17-1
Poetry Harbor
P.O. Box 103
Duluth MN 55801-0103

The author wishes to thank the Anderson Center for Interdisciplinary Studies, where some of these poems were written, and the Minnesota State Arts Board for two grants which allowed for the writing of poems and the preparation of this manuscript.

Acknowledgments:
Great River Review, The Harrisburg Review, Iowa Woman, Mediphors, Nimrod, The North American Review, North Coast Review, Sing Heavenly Muse, Western Journal of Medicine, Windfall, and *The Wolf Head Quarterly.*

Cover Art: Photograph, ©David Bowman, St. Paul, MN

Glacier

In Vedic myth   creation was churned
        from a sea of milk.
How we cling to those first
        gestures of pleasure.
How we swim in that sea
        and the sea   in us
decades before an ice sheet forms
        the weight   accumulating
year by year   the pressure
        increasing   all air space gone
the strength of ice   exceeded by
        the weight of accumulation
until   movement begins
        so slowly   it cannot be seen
a centimeter a day   advancing
        then retreating   advancing.

Something erodes inside:
        the bedrock floor
abraded   polished   the rocky debris
        scraping   as it's pushed along
the rasp in the mind
        unprepared as I am for the unexpected
landslide   for the inevitable
        glacial melt   as unsorted material
is laid at my feet.

Retrieval

1.
I call down birds
call down
a hundred overexcited blackbirds
into a field of crumbling goldenrod
call them one by one
and they keep coming
from such a distance
now everyone will see them
dark and flapping
beyond the west rock wall

2.
steeping a cup of blackberry tea
I watch dried sprigs
unfold in boiling water

burning my tongue
on its bitter taste
I cannot drink down to the leaves
at the bottom of my cup

3.
what stops me
is it the steam
or what comes through it

one bloated leaf
for each delinquent bird
squawking outside my window

they're out there
gleaning the fields
leaping like frogs over stragglers' backs
to advance to the front

alternately
they overtake each other
pieces of a puzzle
that won't stay put

4.
no one speaks of the past

5.
but when the lamp with its warm cheek
goes out
night rushes in
following a path
choked with footsteps
all the way
all the way to my door

6.
afraid of the bed
afraid of the unshaded window
afraid of the door
the wide-open door
afraid of the murky light
the lopsided flowers
a long streak of blood
smeared on the floor

7.
it is my own child's body
curled in her bed

this is the girl I cover
this is the hand
that closes the door
this is the vanished moment
that comes back to me
that I come back to

8.
too numerous to count
with their triggering cries
their skittish motion
blackbirds scatter
then whirl up before
disappearing into pine trees
that bend to balance them

9.
how orderly the world
even the blackest sky
can be contained
by a porcelain cup
the fragile rim
of its horizon

10.
into the brambles
into prickly shrubs of raspberry
and dewberry
into rough bushes of blackberry
with their impenetrable clumps
that arch their backs
along the side of the road
spreading into fence rows
and abandoned meadows and deserted farms
into this world of thorns and juice
I come with the birds
hearts squeaking
squeaking like rusty gates

Mumblety-peg

The knife enters with a dull
thwack as girls take turns
throwing it to the frosty ground.

The knife obeys, burying itself
like a memory sharp enough
to cut through anything to survive.

A hand's throw away,
I wait my turn to retrieve it,
astonished by the wounds

we've made in the earth.
Flinging the black-handled blade
tip down, I watch it split

the shadow looming from my feet.
As I hurry to brush crumbs of dirt
that cling to it, the gleaming steel

waits to be passed on
to the one standing next to me.
How innocently we share

this game with each other;
how deserving the earth seems
to be almost like a body

so we may see
how darkness is cast
face down on the ground.

God's Path

Voices in the wall.
God's fist
cramped in her throat
as she yells.
Christ's blood
splashed everywhere
and glass
like a blown dandelion
dotting the floor.

Wormy fingers
slippery with suds.
Bloody suds
way up in her sleeves.
Snakes
scrolling her arms.
White snakes
bandaging her skin.

Mute walls. Mute
hospital walls.
A needle of fire,
then rags of sleep
unreeling behind her eyes.
Days pass.
Speechless years.

Pink pills
for communion
each morning.
The confessional
every night.
Prudent words
hammered into her:
a woodpecker's
mad beak.
From the radio

a blasphemous sound
fading into a steady
scratch of static.

Finally allowed
to walk outside.
The empty air.
The incurable ennui.
No one to talk to.
No one to hear
the growing trellis
of prayer
climb into
an unsuspecting sky
or to hear voices
in the trees,
voices from every direction.

Night Rain

The rain called to me as it fell:
a splash of noise through the trees,
those endless notes tapping the roof.
It didn't call my sister, not my mother or father,
not even the cat who twitched her tail
whenever it thundered. I couldn't get to sleep.
Beating against a torn screen, it seeped into my room,
soaked the flowered carpet all the way to my bed.
Look at the garden it made–lilies and hyacinth,
bluebells and roses. My feet tiptoed around it.
How quiet I learned to be. How alone.

Sweet Release

        Now and then, after death
a rictus of the facial muscles lifts
the mouth's pinched corners
giving the face the semblance of a smile.

Is it death, then, my mother's
catatonic pose, her stationary body
statue-heavy in a chair? Or is it

the philosopher in her, zigzagging
between the mindless body, the
disembodied mind? Whatever's happened,
she is a corpse to me: arms bent
slightly at the elbow, hands resting
curled against the chest, that bloodless
smile she gives to the kitchen walls
she's stared at six hours now.

        How far she travels
without leaving the room.
No one follows. No need
for food or drink where she's gone.
I kiss her forehead.
She doesn't respond.

Charon's Oboli

Corpse coins.
Coins for a dead man's eyes.
Silver coins laid on motionless lids.
Copper coins under a lead-heavy tongue.
Polished bronze between the deceased's teeth.
Coins to pay the soul's fee to be
Ferried to the realm of the dead.
Money jingles in my pocket. Out of nowhere,
A hand taps my shoulder. Of course
I turn around. Of course I do.

Caduceus

Quoting Athenagorus and Macrobius in support,
Court de Gébelin regarded its gold rod
as symbolizing the equator, the pair of wings
as time, the two serpents—one, male; the other,
female—as Sun and moon threaded together
in opposite directions. Simple enough, but
the scrubbed, freshly-shaven doctor in front of me
shows no interest in this. His desire
is equally simple. He describes the procedure
in clinical terms, the polysyllabic words
cold-blooded as those snakes. Doesn't he see
I miss most of what he says? Doesn't he care
that light and dark are intertwined tightly
as a young girl's braids? Perhaps he's right.
I need to focus. But why has he pinned
a caduceus to his lapel for everyone to see?
Doesn't he give a thought to Hermes or notice
how order moves in a straight line up a phallic staff, surges
toward that medicinal savior, poisonous and braced?

Flashback

Two failures.
Then a third.
A fuss of tubes.

After the doctor is called,
he disappears
between my legs.

The catheter's
rubber lip
inserted into me

inch by inch
burns,
an unrelenting pressure,

the tip pushed
deeper and deeper
until it enters,

the bladder's crypt
opening
for this thief

who picks the lock
of my privacy
and smiles,

not noticing
my voice
change pitch,

panic
chasing across the years.
Blood drains from my face

as I rush back to the place
where my body stopped
being part of me,

and I look down
over myself
at a stranger's legs

being stretched apart.
When it's over
I put on my clothes,

no longer a girl.
The moon's untouchable scar
hovers

outside the window.
I can barely follow
the doctor's anesthetic words,

the bandage he offers,
all the treatments
he has not tried.

Atmosphere

Unmistakable slate-gray clouds
blew in, obscuring the line
between water and sky,
wrapped around the horizon
a gloomy cocoon. Pressing down
over tops of droopy pines, how masterfully
they clapped for my attention.

All night, an unbroken outpouring
I took in like a sponge, and by morning,
water overflowed the gutters,
dripped down the windowpane, leaked
all day from the faucet with the persistence
used to tune an off-key piano:

its *plip   plip   plip   plip*
a fixed rhythm my well-practiced ear
would hear for weeks, for months, for years,
for so many years, I'd float from one
memory to the next down a gushing river
rushing farther and farther into my head.

Homecoming

1. The Mole

The dead mole, its tail,
a toothpick shooting out of its ass,
got raked up into the shovel
I use to collect dog turd. There it was
on the yellow toy snow shovel,
too stiff to evoke any pity
or for me to think too long
about which one of the cats
nailed it in the dirt.
In one grand sweep,
I pitched it into the weeds
that choke a spot behind the barn
where a nesting bird sings.

2. Out the Window

Night thickens into quilled pine.
Two restless scraps of noise
rise from a quivering bush,
while steady ruffles of water
float to my ear. A sagging
net of swallows circles overhead,
and there are rabbits
recklessly thumping in the brush
as wind sings soft-mouthed
into this darkening swirl of sound.

3. After the Nightmare

After the nightmare about a mountain lion
mangling my dog, I wake to feel her
breathing rhythmically at my side, hear

three yellow birds alive in the bush.
The cats stand guard at the window.
We are safe. Sweat dries under my arms.
Like a mirror that absorbs only the surface,
I see blankets and pillows and sun
touch the perfect arc of the dog's spine.
I am amazed at how close the day
comes to me this morning. I'll put
all ten fingers down into stems of grass,
watch the low river, a thread passing through
my life, and later, cut the whitest blossoms,
so that in sleep, I'll dream of my own death
as I drift into one pure curve of snow.

4. At the Shore

No longer summer. The sea
withdraws into itself. There are stars
in the sky, stars soaked in the mud
of this sea. I examine the sucker-tipped
tube feet, the stiff, spiny skin.
Four blunt rays spread out, perfect
as fingers, and another, broken off,
lost somewhere at water's edge.
In the shape of its heavenly body
is my own hand in the universe.
I kneel down, put my mouth to the star
as I would to the body of a man.
Four angels float from my hand,
born of a single kiss. Fluttering
near my cheek, they seem to lift
in the wind, radiate, then settle back
into the solid rays of the starfish. I pray
there is a fifth who can no longer bear
the pain of the world, who is busy
making a new star from a broken piece of arm.

At the Baptism River

after Shimpei Kusano

clouds   motionless mist
    suspended in it
a milk-blue heron
    full-grown wings
        half-erased by
fog but
    breaking through
neck folded
    into an S   wiry legs
        trailing
oh its slow
    flight   over
        the diminishing shore

standing at the Baptism River
    standing
        at the mouth of
and beyond
budding wildflowers
    half-hidden from sight   still
lost to my senses
    lost to
        what doesn't get erased

listen
    from that threshold of trees
loudly
floating out of the ghostly woods
    hon khonk   *hon khonk*
hon khonk   *hon khonk*
listen
I fly from the past
    a bird
        frightened from its nest
no danger
    no hope of return

Corn-Mother

Into the cut and bladed fields
where the last brittle stalks
spoil, rotting on the ground,
where there isn't a trace
of the ghost-white warty gall
that girdled the corn, I walk
by the last row of sheaves
standing stiff in the wind,
swaying, reluctant to die.
The corn-mother waits
in the heart of the field
to be cut into the little doll
I hang in my house each year.
Rescuing her from the plow's
steel teeth, from the reaper
ready to tear her apart,
I give her the shape of a woman–
unthreshed corn transformed
into the mother-sheaf–then scatter
seed from her body to the earth.
Later, I'll wrap her in apron cloth,
place a wreath twined with poppies
atop her head. The golden blades
of hair will trap the sun. All winter,
I will dance at her feet. All winter,
she will celebrate the harvest
beside the framed pictures of saints.

The Oracle

A dance of pebbles in a roadside ditch.
A puddle of water. Hermes on his hands.
God knows what he sees. God knows
this isn't Delphi. I sit waiting on a wall
overrun by greedy vines, listening
to the vocal mark of a grosbeak in brushwood.
I sit waiting, my ear an arrow hunting
that bird. What to do? Where
to go next? The future is stubborn.
It resists my questions, hardens
into a handful of rocks, mute at my feet,
black as newly-ripened berries
gleaming straight at me through the woods.

The Ear of the Owl

1.
Low moans start up in the pine
like soft bird cries
as we lie together in love.
I listen to the wind
with an owl in its mouth.

2.
If an owl is slain,
its heart pulled out and laid
on the left breast
of a sleeping woman,
the woman
will talk in her sleep,
revealing all her secrets.

3.
I sent my soul to hide
in the owl's breast. Now,
bird of my spirit,
see how my life
is bound to you,
and by guarding you,
how I protect all the lives
of the women I love.

4.
When I touch her breasts,
a velvet ruff of feathers
slides beneath me. I cross
to the other side of myself.
When I leave, I imitate
the noiseless flight of an owl.

5.
When the white moon rises,
I disappear into the woods,
offer my body to the owl,
uncovering my soft throat,
my white feathered breast.
I fall into her, tuck my head
under her wing, and I sleep.
When I wake, I find myself
changed back into a woman.

6.
The goddess Athena
was given the shape
of an owl with breasts.
Egyptians called Isis *Athene*:
I have come from myself.

7.
Each dark act
must find its song.

8.
A woman touching
another woman–
the owl calling us
to the wisdom of that first
raw second of arousal.

9.
In the growing funnel of dusk,
I offer my words
to the ear of the owl.
A woman's eyes
shine back at me.
Her song, in a sudden
rush inside of me,
rises, opening out
like a fountain's
sweet water, flowing
out into the dark
current of the world.

The White Bridge
for C.

Don't be afraid of the white space
between words. Cross it. Follow
the arching silence. If asked, stop–
even if it's before the word
chasm, even if you're suspended
between *trauma* and *change*,
even though your body halts
for a split second between the steel
brace of words. Don't be afraid.
Dare to leap that pencil-thin bridge

between stanzas. You will have to
look down. Don't worry. Heights frighten
almost everyone. I promise you'll be safe.
It'll feel like solid ground underneath.
Go ahead, relax.
Let yourself breathe.
Lean all the way forward
and with your quietest gaze, observe
the indolent space between these mountains.
And when the ropes sag in your hands,
ask yourself the eternal questions.
Do you see the crude cliffs, the snaking scar
water makes on the world below?
What does your life look like from here?

Fracture

Coastal mountains break off into ravines,
forming a three-pointed coronet–steep fault scarps
dropping off, the downward buckling, invaginated rocks–
then from those unfathomable depths, volcanic cones rise
thousands of feet into sky, rise like the sun before it slides
back into night, or like a lover, uplifted and adorned,
but eventually lost in the thrust down, the dizzying fall.
The weak heart crumbles. A rift widens
into the drop-off we fear. Seven million years
should teach us how naturally earth
strains toward a summit then has to collapse,
how the doomed heights cannot hold, how
any crown we wear is restless on our heads.

The Hive

1.
In winter, I tunnel through snow.
In spring, it's the plow.
A thousand cuts in the field.
In summer, a thorn
scrapes a bloody furrow in my skin.
Ditches fill with color.
Trees, once green, go bare to the top.
My feet make a trench in the leaves
as an insistent bee
rises from the underbrush.
Does it expect to soothe me
when it kisses my hand?

2.
I wanted you
as no one has ever wanted me,
but I waited
while the first gray hairs
appeared on my head,
waited for the stars'
glacial drift around a snowy comet
that comes once a century,
its fading tail
luminous as fishline,
waited for the other woman
to die or divorce,
waited long after I refused.
I was left waiting
while bees hummed in their hives
and winter choked
the river's throat with ice.

3.
Amid green thumbs of weeds,
a most common flower
sends up from masses of dark,
deeply-cut leaves, tall blue blossoms.
Just opened, it lures a visiting bee
that zigzags flower to flower,
disappears inside a petal's puckered skirt.
Eurydice, I think. When I turn, a head
powdered with white pollen emerges,
and the shadow mine makes
moves plant by plant around the garden.

4.
What else could I do
the day I found
lying motionless on the sill
the plump corpse of a bee?
I held it in my hand.
Cradling its velvet-coated body,
I noticed my own lifeline,
an arrow underneath it,
while outside, toiling bees
crisscrossed in the sun.
Consider the bee and see how she labours.

5.
Everywhere in the exotic
flowering of that garden, bees
soared and hovered, wings
beating the air, heart-shaped heads
visible on honeysuckle and catkins
collecting acres of pollen, the world
astir around me. It was there,
between the dense notes of your pulse,
you kissed me, bewildered
about where to place this moment
given our complicated lives.
Days later the tremor you sent through me

returned: the aftershock of bees
drawing nectar to make
a single drop of honey.

6.
Look at the beehive you've made of my heart
Look at the swarm clustering around me
    and the wax I use
    trying to seal myself off
Look at what you've become
    a bear
    clumsy and mulish
Look at yourself
    nosing the feathery ferns
    the milky-colored mushrooms
    ignoring the dizzy funnel of bees at your back
Look at the muscles bunch in your legs
    then stretch the long length of a tree
Look at your claws thrusting toward me
    your muzzle smeared
    by the dripping honey
Look at me tremble
Look at the paper-thin comb
    wedged between my ribs
Look at it
    then tell me again how the wind you miss
    sleeps in my hair
    again
    about the tangled hues in my eyes.

7.
Inhabited by bees.
Spring still burning in my eyes.
The intricate dance
home from the flower.
In my deepest thoughts,
the smell of the hive.

I surrender to it all.

My heart is thick with pleasure,
but I'll tell you
about the holes inside,
the honeycomb
I've worked for years to fill.

8.
A secluded nest
and bees
breathing beneath my ribs.
A scent of clover in the air.
Certain summer nights
love comes to me
frantic for meaning.
I haven't got the answer,

but I know how honey
sweetens the tongue,
how my own blood hums
from the bee's nimble bite.

9.
First the swarm tone
then a dense cloud
forming, the impetuous flight
to limb or random stump,
fence or ladder where bees
alight. Are these the ones
Aristaeus saw sicken and die,
that touched the lips of Pindar
and Plato as they lay helplessly
in their cradles, that crossed
the lips of St. Ambrose
before entering his mouth?

10.
The greedy bee
returning to its hive
with sticky feet, a packed pollen basket,
looks half-drunk from venturing
beyond the petal's crease
and into the trumpet-throated lily
left drooping on the garden wall.
It drones, the same sound
that flows through my veins
as we sleep, side by side
across a continent, our words
holding us together like the thin
cells of a hive. Is this the unhesitating life
I was meant to lead?
Many chambers? Much noise?

11.
From my pursed mouth,
a single word
works its way out
like a pillow feather
then floats to the floor,

but I'm not ready for the truth,
cannot ask who or when or why.
Why bother with explanations
when my tongue is dead in my mouth,
and bees half-crazed in my head.

I stare out at a frozen landscape,
at moonlit gardens of ice
spreading over the fields,
at a fraction of light, so far off,
shining at me from the other side.

12.
A hum of bees from dry lips
all night in my ear:
a swarm of words inside a crimson flower.

It clings to me–the sugary
smear of honey on my hands,
pollen dusting my breast.

What frightens me awake,
lighting a flame deep in my cheek?

I fly out of myself,
all that we love between us.

13.
I open the window,
and night blows in
thin bandages of fog.

Something tears in my chest.

So much for my dreams.
They back out of the room
on tiptoe.

14.
Only when they'd sensed
thick puffs of smoke
filling the hive
did those feral bees forget
their tending and ready
themselves to abandon it.

Once gorged on honey,
too full to bend into
stinging position for defense,
the docile workers forgot
how singlemindedly they'd returned
from the snow asters in the field.

Spooked by fire
from a smoldering bee smoker
that smelled of pine needles
and sumac bobs, they ate their way
into a stupor while the beekeeper
cut that dead limb and carried it away.

15.
When your letter appeared,
I held it for an hour, remembering
the way our bodies joined
one last time to say good-bye.
I couldn't write for a month,
my words falling off the page
as I stared at snow swirling
a thousand miles between us.
Not even a warm day
could woo me into the world
to watch the bees' brief
thistledown flight.
You never wrote again, but
I will tell you now about memory,
the crust it formed
so I could heal,
the scab I picked
until it bled.

16.
For months winter disguised it—
the hidden hive body
nobody touched—but after spring
melted the last snow from my hand
and all that was unsaid
vanished in a river of water,
the slow-headed bees
dropped from the comb
one by one, half-starved,
the colony so strong

they'd run out of food
weeks before any flowers would bloom.
I put out pots of sugared syrup
to save them. It was only a matter of time.
How could I stop those clumsy,
richly-veined wings from stirring inside?

17.
How sharply the thorn stuck in my finger,
how reliable my blood
making its own rose in my hand,

and this memory of you:

the withered petal
the flower didn't feel
when it fell.

Signs

Our love had left its mark
by the time you went away:

a wilted Christmas wreath
hanging cockeyed on the door,

a cat-stained cushion I smelled
then rushed to wash,

even that old car with its
expanding sweater of rust.

The signs were everywhere,
yet everywhere I looked I saw you.

If pintail ducks rose
in pairs from the river,

or outside an unlatched window
a mourning dove's voice

bared its defeated heart
to anyone who'd listen,

I'd long for the world to be
just the world again,

for birds to sing to birds,
for the ducks' wishbone flight.

Second Sight

1.
Found stunned northside of Townline Road,
the snowy owl drove boxed in my car
two hours to reach the raptor volunteer
who held the half-blind bird overnight
then rode four more hours before
delivering it, disoriented,
to a steel table where men
took a silver scalpel to its head.

2.
In my cupped hand, the real
fruit of Eden: smooth, leathery,
thick-skinned, forbidden for its
crimson juice, thin vesicles,
dripping pulp. The venous-
colored seed Persephone welcomed
into her mouth. It was the owl
perched at the threshold of Hell
who saw her swallow, who
denounced her for obediently
swallowing. It was the owl.

3.
A deep sweetness on the tongue.
The simple *yes* I give
to the things I love.

4.
Thrashing in the closed
coffin of that box, the owl punched
holes in old cardboard where
the hooked beak broke through.
Specks of blood and battered feathers
littered the makeshift nest.

No matter the effort,
wings failed to bring it to flight.

5.
Over the pitched spine of an abandoned barn,
a ghostly owl, over
snow rows and fence posts,
over chips of bottle glass flashing
in a ditch and the deserted
undiminished miles,
over the emotional weight of that road,
it crosses straight out in front of me,
and the car so accurate as it skids
on ice, slides trunk-first into a tree.

6.
Where the moon has been shining,
a predatory eye
and something breathing
beyond the gate where the cemetery lies.

7.
Like pond lilies floating open,
unspoiled feathers
drape my gloved hand,
but I feel claws leafing out,
gripping me, not wanting to let go.
Behold the convulsive dive,
the heartstopping drop as it breaks
a crust of snow to take exactly what it wants.

8.
A savage, unlucky creature,
the Chinese say, terrifying
because it devours the mother.
Yet how do you judge one

that eats what it sees,
sees what it eats?

9.
The moon: no light of its own--
it is all reflection.

10.
Those milky wings hunt me
into the night as if I were harmless
as a field mouse or tree frog
offering nothing
but a penny of consciousness
as it dies. My eyes close.
I whirl down,
a tide of bones at my feet.

11.
One eye changes places
with another. The owl swivels its neck,
sees me with one good eye. A moon appears,
and I float there, my reflection
gliding in icy light. There I am
fully seen for the first time.
There I am, fingers brushing its neck–
out of foolishness or arrogance
or grace–stroking it as I would
a lover's brow, touching my lips
to the dangerous pillow of its head.

After Visiting a Nature Conservancy Volunteer

Driving north through Wisconsin, past Lulu Lake,
the Muckwonago River, I recited her list of pests:
bindweed, burdock, leafy sponge,
pondweed, milfoil, plumeless thistle,
identified the scenery as I went—fen, sedge meadow,
bog, shrub-carr—stopped to watch cricket frogs
and Cooper's hawks, filled the lakes with bluegill,
spotted bass, long-eared sunfish, star-headed
minnows, filled the woods with hickory and hackberry,
paper birch, let my tongue roll over tussock bulrush,
northern kittentail, Blandings' turtles, thought about
how language cries out for a subject, how self
and subject merge in the black-bibbed sparrow,
the honeybee wooed from a brimming hive,
the triumphant pokeweed tasseled in white.

Deciphering the Alphabet

1.
Winter advances
leaving its white tracks
scampering through the woods,
through the barren fields,
over the three hills
I climb each December
to get to the river
where velvety shrews
and voles and squirrels
crisscross in the snow,
their claw marks
reminding me of the exquisitely
complicated pattern
I watched an old Indian
bite into birchbark.
(*Art as old as the world*,
the woman said to me.)

2.
In the origin myth of Eskimos
the first children
sprouted from fertile soil
like tender plants,
stayed rooted there,
being nourished by the earth.
No one knows how one boy and one girl
grew into adults
able to walk away
into the world,
to meet and marry.

3.
Each tree
was a letter once.
Pagans

spelled out their secrets
by threading
the proper leaves
in proper order–
Birch tree, Heather leaf,
leaf of the Ash.
Forests of possibility.
A language
you could hold in your hand.
Words that quivered,
turned color in the fall,
that could be taken back,
burned in regret.
Lonely winters
when there was nothing
to say.

4.
From a north window
the choked river,
a slippery crack of light.
Does she notice me
crouched down,
my bare fingers exploring
deer tracks I've found,
some chips in the ice?
I wave once,
but she stares
absentmindedly into the cold.
Pure imitation.
The great bored glacier of her face.

5.
How many have known
the endless emptiness
inside an ordered room?
How many, a silence
so profound, inside
and out?

6.
I turn, startled,
as if someone
dogged my steps.
Nothing.
Midday sun
scatters down
among towering spruce.
At my feet, birdtracks
wherever I look.
The only ciphers of the day.
My footprints merge
with the ones laid down here,
my whole body,
heart, lung, muscle,
leaving its trace.

7.
Everything that moves
leaves a story. No story
can exist by itself.

8.
What am I to the wolf,
rabbit and fox?
To those songless birds
balancing on branches?
To the solitary pines
dipped in frost?

9.
First the trough
where it plowed forward,
then the wide belly-slide
down the bank,
the musty scent-post,
the scat, the smooth hole

where the otter slipped
through a window in the ice.
Scattered all around,
a wolverine's fresh tracks,
a slash where claws raked
as it slid to a stop.
Stiff gusts of wind
kick up around me.
Twigs and bits of debris
soon mar the tracks.
Before long, the sharp edges
will begin to slump.
By early next week,
everything will be erased,
the immaculate snow
unable to keep the shape
of a single creature.

About the Author:

This is Francine Sterle's first poetry collection. A native of Minnesota, she holds a Master of Fine Arts degree in poetry from Warren Wilson College and has studied writing in a variety of settings, including Oxford University in Oxford, England, the Spoleto Writers' Workshop in Spoleto, Italy, the Bread Loaf Writers' Conference, the Atlantic Center for the Arts, and the Squaw Valley Community of Writers. Awards include a Lake Superior Contemporary Writers Award, a Loft-McKnight Foundation Award, a Pushcart Prize nomination, a residency fellowship from the Anderson Center for Interdisciplinary Studies, a Jerome Foundation Travel and Study Grant, as well as both a Fellowship Grant and a Career Opportunity Grant from the Minnesota State Arts Board. Her poems have been published in such literary journals as *The North American Review, Nimrod, CutBank, Atlanta Review, Birmingham Poetry Review, The Beloit Poetry Journal, Zone 3*, and many others. Francine has also taught workshops and classes in venues ranging from The Depot to the Range Mental Health Center to the University of Minnesota. She currently resides in the tiny Iron Range town of Cherry, Minnesota.